A Credible Universe

Poems of faith

Simon Baynes

with a Foreword by David Winter

Cover illustration by Fay Peters

A Credible Universe
Poems of Faith,
by Simon Baynes.

Published by Moorend Press
23 Moorend Lane
Thame
Oxon. OX9 3BQ.

First published in November 2002.

ISBN 0-9543692-0-3

Copies are obtainable from the above address, price £6, postage free.

50p. from every copy sold will be donated to Tearfund.

Printed by MP Printers Ltd.
Unit C10
Station Road
Thame
Oxon.

© Simon Baynes 2002.

FOREWORD

by the Rev Canon David Winter, former Head of Religious Broadcasting, BBC, writer and broadcaster

Poetry is about intensity: intensity of feeling and intensity of language. Time and again when writers have wanted to deal with the deepest of human emotions they have turned to poetry as a way of expressing it. Economy of language – good poetry is seldom long-winded! - and evocative images can often evoke feelings beyond the reach of prose. I have read many of Simon Baynes' poems and heard him reading some of them. He is certainly never long-winded! But he is a poet who shows in language and imagery that he is at home with the medium. He deals in pictures and ideas, making connections between things we see, feelings we experience and questions we ask. This is genuine poetry.

One of the remarkable features of the modern artistic world is the revival of writing and reading poetry, an idea some critics would have scoffed at twenty years ago. Ordinary people turn their inexpert hands to it when faced with deep emotions they wish to express. More and more writers find themselves preferring the medium of poetry to prose – and more and more people are reading it. Simon is typical of a small army of what we might call 'locality poets', who help to earth this revival in the lives of friends and neighbours, and in familiar scenes and settings.

I hope many people will enjoy this latest selection of his work. I believe they will.

TEAR FUND

The Evangelical Alliance Relief Fund was founded in 1968 as a Christian relief and development charity, working to bring help and hope to communities in need around the world.

In 2001 it supported 643 projects in more than 80 countries in disaster response, aid relief, basic needs (e.g. clean water), health, education, micro-enterprise and advocacy.

Tearfund has particular expertise in working through indigenous churches as agents for change, though its beneficiaries are by no means exclusively Christian; they belong to all faiths or none.

Tearfund employs 182 full-time, 32 part-time and 45 sessional staff. Its income in 2001-2002 was £32.8 million.

For further information, or to make a donation, write to:
 Tearfund
 Freepost
 Teddington
 Middlesex
 TW11 8BR.

> Tel: 0845 355 8355.
> Email: enquiry@tearfund.org
> Web: www.tearfund.org.

**TO THE WORKERS AND PARTNERS
OF TEAR FUND AROUND THE WORLD**

Following the simple
word, they go
armed with nothing
but the Spirit's sword,
God's promise. The deal

is simple, nothing can
gainsay such trust.
They go with the charge
to tell creation,
to save and heal.

Seeds of hope
drills and ploughs
with the Spirit's
gift of patience
are their business;

the farmer's eye
for weather, hand
for the break of soil,
bringing Jesus the poor man
to the poor in their distress.

Cooking pots for Goma
salvation and radishes
for Guatemala;
drains and wells in
Sierra Leone;

Asylum seekers in
Ilford find
love, the surprise, when
the everlasting Father
seeks his own.

Petitions for Ian
Stillman, sand filters
for Ethiopia
blankets and bakeries
for Afghanistan

say to hurt people
to the despairing
"I can do all things
through him who strengthens me".
I can, I can.

They have for hero
the man of sorrows
who drove back the darkness
bearing in his hands
the world's nails;

the undefeated
whose song endures
beyond all discord
till the ultimate kingdom
of love prevails.

CONTENTS

Part I A CREDIBLE UNIVERSE – Poems of Creation

A Duty
Civilisation
Five Haiku on Creation
A Ham
Two Pictures
May Morning
Thoughts in a Greenhouse
Poplars
Power Failure
Old Chestnut
Turning
A Hard Frost
Evidence
Wedding
Why Beauty?

Part II THIS STRIDING EDGE – Poems of the Life of Faith

Shipwreck
Palm Sunday Meditation
Praise
The Argument
Bible Reading
The Littleness of Evil
Yes
Image
Why not Joy?
On reading Stevie Smith
Thoughts of a Christian turned Fifty
Spots
Edge
Rook
Wall
A Better Country

Children of the King
Ballad of the King's Children
Reading John
On a Desert Island

Part III WE ARE HIS POEM – Poems of People and Places

Freed
Abnormal Child
Little Gidding
Keep Britain Tidy
Jesus Christ, Poet
For Bemerton
At the Frontier
Flop
A Carol for St Nicholas
Morning After the Election, 6am
Absolutely Always
We will Rejoice
Dome's Day
Sheltered Accommodation
Sixteen
Joshua Chapter 3
Three Children of the King
Truth and Beauty

Part IV COMING HOME – Poems of Time and Eternity

Apocalypse
Humph
One Way
Crown Him Lord of All
Here He Comes
Superficial
Time
Commonly Called Life
The Stream of Time

Part 1

A CREDIBLE UNIVERSE

Poems of creation

A DUTY

"The poet has a duty to love and to praise"
                          Cecil Day Lewis, *The Poet's Task*
            Inaugural lecture as Professor of Poetry at Oxford, 1951.

I praise
praise.

Yes, we have had
too much of it, from
Wordsworth worshipping
Blea Tarn or whatever
to Stevie Smith
even Stevie Smith
adoring
the slumbering
Humber.

And I could add
a hundred names.

But praise
gives meaning
and dignity
to the frame of things;

sings, like Caedmon,
creation, and makes
a credible universe.

CIVILISATION

Sparrows in
the Saturday
street approve
a market economy

   A consortium
   of starlings
   debate a
   share issue.

      Housing is
      top of the
      agenda for
      the long-tailed tit.

         A mother
         thrush
         introduces the
         education bill.

            How the
            cuckoos
            maintain their
            telecommunications!

               Robins have
               their territorial
               disputes, their
               border fighting.

Eggs are
easy pickings
hi-jacked
by daws.

> Honour the
> black-backed
> gull, upwardly
> mobile.

*

Strange how we
parrot them, the
sixth day being after
the fifth day.

FIVE HAIKU ON CREATION

Adam's eye opened.
How he must have stared and stared!
How God must have smiled.

Look, the gritty sand
every grain a little world.
There's a miracle!

Laughter rings in heaven.
That's the duck-billed platypus!
It's April the first.

Peas, now; take the pea.
What designer could have made
something so absurd?

Look, leviathan!
look, behemoth! Now I see
Lord, now I believe.

A HAM

A ham
a hammer
and a hamadryad
are three
very different
things.

Which only
goes to show
how very confusing
but also rather
mysterious
and wonderful
life is.

TWO PICTURES

Such a rarity:

the meticulous printing
of branches against
a dawn of wild colours
dated January
inland; three hundred
black seagulls wheeling
the time seven thirty;

and at nine
three hundred white
seagulls grounded
in a green washed meadow;
the same gulls;
the same day.

MAY MORNING

I like the little green rows, still neat
punctuating the damp soil, the inch high
semi-colons of beans spaced in order;

carrots a line of exclamation
marks, tight in their form.

Though chickweed and vetch misprint
my trim paragraph, I the compositor mind
my peas like question marks uncurling.

Look! Here's a dotted line of lettuce
no higher than Tom Thumb; here's
a flourish, a demanding marrow,
a vivid cucumber, an ampersand;

tomatoes in this dawn, illuminated
capitals proudly standing;
rubrics are radishes.

Hoeing and raking
such nice orthography, such
syntactical eight-point splendour, I tend
to admire the mysterious author.

THOUGHTS IN A GREENHOUSE

    Not content
With every food of life to nourish man,
By kind illusions of the wondering sense
Thou mak'st all Nature beauty to his eye.
        Mark Akenside, *Pleasures of the Imagination*, III 489.

It was not necessary
for God to create
several thousand hairs
on the stem of a tomato plant
which standing between
the morning mid July
seven o'clock sun
and the eye, dazzle
with more than Solomon's
glory; not, one would think,
a prerequisite of fruit,
tomato's or my
survival. Creation
could have been otherwise.

POPLARS

In stillest air
the sycamore stands
dormant; in the broad leaves
nothing is doing.
One would say they had
forgotten their being.
But the poplar leaves
are endlessly
twisting and turning.

The oak tree, conscious
of its calling, waits
the coming centuries
complacently, having
no need to remember
this particular day.
But the poplar leaves
unawed by history
are quietly laughing.

Even the birch tree
flags no wind
seeming to signal
with its tiny leaves
a season of sleep.
The garden birdsong
is lazy. But still
the poplar tree
goes dancing on.

POWER FAILURE ON A SUMMER NIGHT

By moonlight and candlelight
 strangely content
this still night, this Sunday night
 we sit a quiet hour.
Cicadas never change their tune;
 then why should we lament
the loss of such far-fetched and
 unnecessary power?

Rather, in a rash moment –
 hearing what the frogs say
we would renounce the power that perhaps
 was a failure anyway,
if only by this act we might
 true power, true life discover,
and moonlight and candlelight
 be ours for ever.

OLD CHESTNUT

Unfathomable grace, grace upon grace
that the same chestnut which surprised our childhood
in May with such munificence of flame
should punctually expend, year after year
its prodigal whiteness to delight our children
and teach them beauty.

    More: that its bursting shells,
the oldest joke in nature, after such years
should scatter conkers down to satisfy
my sons and me and all October boys,
one tree, all generations; grace on grace
and of his fulness have all we received.[1]

---

[1] John 1.16. Cf. "We all live off his generous bounty,
   gift after gift after gift" – Eugene Peterson, *The Message*

TURNING

As my birch

turns the corner

into November

I too defy

coming death;

prepare for spring;

flame into praise.

A HARD FROST

Written for the new millennium, December 1999,
on the theme of "Brave New World"

A hard frost grips the land. Thistle and dock
start from grey corners; waste and rubble strew
the abandonned yard; nettle and feverfew,
elder and bindweed, smother heaps of rock

in drab disorder, taunting us to find
some brave pre-vision of a better day
for our new century; a surer way
for man and nature to fulfil their kind.

But since the frost, clothing the thistle seed,
is gloried by the winter sun aslant,
we have as much as we can bear of bliss.

We cannot ask more beauty, cannot need
a greater miracle; we cannot want
a braver, or a newer, world than this.

EVIDENCE

If I observe, as I may
how the overlapping of clouds
the motorway lanes
and the petals of a rose
fold, as they do, one into another
the case for life is proved.

Never can there be
ground for despair;
fulness of life
cannot be gainsaid;
and all the promises of God
are yes and amen.[1]

---

[1] II Corinthians 1.20

WEDDING

A wedding is going on.

The organ thunders
pomp and circumstance
playing for me
audience of one.

The wedding of earth and air
wedding of heart and leaf
wedding of time and flower
wedding of the one and the all
wedding of self and sound.

God takes his place
in the silence following
the statement of empire.

Practice is over.

Life begins here.

WHY BEAUTY?

Why beauty exists at all? Is that a question
any philosopher asks?

Granted we are spinning
to destruction; for the news
and the documentaries hammer it home.
The tale of everyday disasters
quickens. The world-scale horrors, the man-made
spoiling of nature, clap a condemned
notice on our familiar habitat.
Space is littered with explodable junk.[1]

The crescendo is just
beginning. Moreover we love
our doomed home, and have not skill or will
to jump to the next available lodging place –
humanity set to become a refugee
without a refuge.

    Why then
must the birch tree (this is only the first
random thing to appear)
print its semiquavers on the common
seven o'clock sky; why should clouds
(clouds, so unnecessary)
endlessly enrich and satisfy?

No one can answer. We shall never know
why beauty exists. Or why we desire it.

---

[1] There are said to be over 23,000 pieces of debris larger than a cricket ball floating in space, the collision of any two of which could be catastrophic.

Part 2

THIS STRIDING EDGE

Poems of the life of faith

SHIPWRECK

We spread full sail
and ran before the wind
a glorious voyage of discovery
a maiden trip.

Our ship was sound, we thought;
her figurehead Jesus
and her name Faith.

We did not see the rock.

Our wreck was sudden and immediate
our loss was absolute.

After the first shock we cry
Where were you, Jesus?
You were not on watch
you were not at the helm
we have lost you utterly –

unless
unless
you yourself are the rock.

PALM SUNDAY MEDITATION

" 'His virtue makes him mad' [Byron on DonQuixote]. There is a profound truth in this. It was their virtue that made Christ, St Francis, Blake, Daruma, all mad, mad as hatters, compared to sane people like you and me."
>RH Blyth, *Zen in English Literature.*

"The glorious madness of God."
>GA Studdert Kennedy.

What was it all for, that mad donkey ride?
What kind of a smile on the face of the master?
 Of patient sorrow?
 or irony?
        or giddy triumph?
lost in wonder love and praise?
drunk with excitement?

Mad for a moment? Yes, magnificently mad
 for two days at least.
Mad at this pigeon-selling world,
its enclosure of seats and cages,
having come from many days' march on muddy roads.

Here was a second transfiguration,
 one in the eye for Peter, James and John
 of which they missed the point.

They preferred him preaching in the hills
 to marching in the streets.
They preferred the other kind of demonstration.

He is mad, after all, they must have thought,
with the whiplash in his hand.

You must be mad, master, said earnest Judas,
You are going about it all the wrong way.

Mad, murmured the priests
 looking down from behind curtains,
 and must be removed.

These Jews, said Pilate, they drive me mad.

And two days later the divine wrath passed on
 like a meteor which they had missed.
Only the fig tree knew.

We usually side
 with Peter, James and John,
 Judas, and Pilate.

We prefer
 religion and politics unmad.

We go back
 to the curtained
 predictable
 sedentary
 money-changing
 world.

PRAISE

At the top of my voice
I will praise God,
the top of my voice
which is the place
of anger, pride and pain.

From the bottom of my heart
I will praise God,
the bottom of my heart
which is the place
of every mortal sin.

THE ARGUMENT

"My world, what a beauty!
(though I say it)" God said.
"Revenge!" howled the devil
 as he fell on his head.
"My law" said the Lord
and he planted a pippin.
 "A snare" thought the tempter
 "for Adam to trip in".
"Salvation!" cried God
"through the people I choose".
 Satan nearly died laughing.
 "The Jews! God, the Jews!"
Then "Moses" frowned God.
 The destroyer quipped "Aaron!"
"Quails and manna to feast on."
 "A gold calf to swear on."
"Well, Joshua."
 "Achan!"
"The judges."
 "Delilah!"
"A king!" challenged God.
 "Saul!" answered the smiler.
So "Prophets! I have it,
my prophets!" God cried.
 "I'm a prophet myself"
 Satan said. (But he lied.)
 Then "Babylon, Babylon,
 lions, and fire"
 he gloated. "Why doesn't God
 send the messiah?
 The eagle, the legions,
 the tribute, the yoke –

his majesty certainly
seems to be broke!…
What? shepherds? What? Rumours?
What? Messages heard?"
"My son!" said the Father
"and that's my last word!"

BIBLE READING

Because of time and time
and time again I turn
where daily lies the word
with even-handed page.

From fear to faith I wander
between its wrath and ruth
to action or to passion
between its peace and rage.

Soft-selling promises
have in their heart to woo me
with love and nothing matters
fear not and all is well

but the hammer and the fire and the lightning
flash and the sword cry woe
do not travel that road too lightly
soft is the road to hell.

Because of time and chance
I follow word for word.
the rock that rests for ever
the straw that dances kindly,

the throne with jewels set
the world where poor men die
I cling to both for answer
and, if it must be, blindly.

THE LITTLENESS OF EVIL

If we could once see light
as indeed the first created thing
brightly irrupting from all edges
of the compass to the heart, soft
to the touch, lively as unfolding petals,
holding all colours in its cup,

we might know how it was
that the devil came sneaking in
with a little black candle
and planted his flames of darkness
as the droppings of a weasel
smudge a field of snow.

Then we should see at last
how alien, how utterly other
and unnatural, also how sickly
and breakable, and in the end
how unimportant, these bastard
germs of darkness are.

YES

Somewhere between paradox
 and platitude lies
  the true and beautiful.

Between peace and peacemaking
 passion and passing
  runs the road.

Between dawn and daylight
 fire and frying pan
  our way is often.

We are speechless because
 between yes and yes
  is the answer.

IMAGE

Caesar
and money
go together.

He prints
his image
on little
round
pieces of
copper.

Let him
keep it.

God prints
his image
on me.

WHY NOT JOY?
    … miss
Of life, just at the gates of life and bliss.
                        George Herbert, *The Sacrifice*

We might be otherwise – we might be all
We dream of happy, high, majestical.
Where is the love, beauty and truth we seek
But in our mind? and if we were not weak
Should we be less in deed than in desire?
                        Shelley, *Julian and Maddalo*

Surely there was a time I might have trod
The sunlit heights…
                            Oscar Wilde, *Helas!*

    O to be free,
To burn one's old ships!
                            Ib., *The Burden of Itys*

With such stars to guide us – the very word
of God, the very body of Christ, the very plan
of our happiness – all this given, what goes wrong?
Once say yes, and surely blessing follows?

Only one act of will, only seek first
the kingdom, and everything falls into place?
But we learn true love, though seen, is not so sudden;
paradise here, but not so easy to come by.

Why may we not say yes? We are kept going
on little stabs of joy, and the softer pleasures;
the need to keep going; what people will think.

Could we not once step clear of all this
like the bellying of a grounded parachute
and begin to walk barefoot on our native grass?

ON READING STEVIE SMITH

"Death lies in our hands; he must come if we call him."
    Stevie Smith, *What poems are made of* (1969), et passim.

The trouble with suicide
as a way of life
is that you can never
never never never never (Lear)
never again
ever
eat
strawberries and cream.

Not even strawberries.

In heaven
sheol, hades
valhalla
nirvana
purgatory, limbo
nothingness
or paradise
(even paradise)
they are
not served.

It is
a solemn
decision
to make.

THOUGHTS OF A CHRISTIAN TURNED FIFTY

The score is not impressive;
my boots pinch
but I am still on the field
muddy but unbowed.[1]

With so many missed chances
bungled tackles
and own goals
it is a wonder my manager
has not yet called me in.

But here I am
into the second half
under the glare of the crowd
keeping my captain[2]
in the corner of my eye.

Sometimes even now
passes come my way.
Steady it.

There is, of course, the Cup.[3]

I hope the whistle
will find me
pressing
towards the goal.[4]

---

[1] An echo of WE Henley's "bloody but unbowed".
[2] See Hebrews 12.2.
[3] "Cup" has a double meaning for Christians: blessing, as in Psalm 23, but also trial, testing, suffering, as in Mark 14.36.
[4] See Philippians 3.14.

SPOTS

Thank goodness

the leopard

can't change

his spots.

Thank goodness

God can

change

mine.

EDGE

Lord, if you are not there
what emptiness
opens at our feet.

The ground is dangerous.

Unfathered we walk
this striding edge.

And how alone
we are
in our crowded streets.

ROOK

I perch on life
like an old rook
on a dead branch
of the acacia tree.

We peck
whatever joy
we can from the
crumbling bark.

We know to the bone
its rottenness,
rook and I.
We hear it crack.

We grieve
for other birds
who have no hope.
But we have wings.

Written on seeing a rook on the dead branch of
an acacia tree in the churchyard, before taking
the funeral of an 18 year- old boy.
"Brothers, we do not want you… to grieve
like the rest of men, who have no hope."
I Thessalonians 4.13.

WALL

With the help of my God I shall leap over the wall.
                    Psalm 18.29 (Book of Common Prayer)

People face walls
students checking results
bad Victorian children
soldiers to be frisked

pachinko players
the Wall Street walkers
the large-bottomed[1]
at their cash machines.

People face walls
Hezekiah lamenting[2]
men to pee
and Jews to pray.

With the help
of my God
I shall leap over
the wall.

---

[1] *Large-bottomed* was the term used by GH Hardy the mathematician for 'the confident, booming, imperialist, bourgeois English'. (CP Snow, *Variety of Men* p.46)
[2] Isaiah 38.2

A BETTER COUNTRY

If they had been thinking of the country they had left, they would have had opportunity to return. Instead, they were longing for a better country – a heavenly one.

Hebrews 11.16

Travelling hopefully
became too much of a creed.

The plans never quite came good.
Extravagant hopes that one day
a grand simplicity would emerge
from intractible matter, eluded fulfilment.

Annus mirabilis was always
next year, and never broke. Splendour
amassed, but failed to peak.
Dying, he looked for a better country.

This loser was, shall we say,
something of a winner after all.

A common thought. Compare:

Hope springs eternal in the human breast.
Man never is, but always to be blest.

Pope.

Effort and expectation and desire
And something evermore about to be.

Wordsworth.

Great is the facile conqueror;
Yet haply he, who, wounded sore,
Breathless, unhorsed, all cover'd o'er
 With blood and sweat,
Sinks foiled, but fighting evermore,
 Is greater yet.

                                                William Watson.

Stagnation is what I fear; adventure and failure are far, far better.

                                                Ottoline Morrell.

[*The Battle of Maldon*] In those days too poets preferred heroic failure to brilliant success.

                                                John Bayley.

CHILDREN OF THE KING

His stride was regal.
When he called for followers
a movement was born.
Men gave their hearts to him.
He said, let the children come.

They built castles
drunk with greatness
creating a cabinet
of future power.
I wanted children, he said.

Schemes of revolution
darkened the landscape.
Whispered plots were discovered.
Swords flashed and failed.
They ran away like children.

Total defeat
followed. And then he came
at dawn, invincible love
making all the difference.
Children, do you love me? he said.

The movement began.

THE BALLAD OF THE KING'S CHILDREN

King Richard sat in his council hall;
 affairs of state were done.
His nobles jested and took their ease
 at the time of the setting sun,

when the grave Lord Ranger made his way
 to the presence of the king.
"My lord, what is it that troubles your mirth,
 and who are these you bring?"

"Pray pardon me, my sovereign liege,
 but justice I would see.
These felons were found in the King's greenwood
 and they took no heed of me,

but with bold despite they laid an axe
 to the root of a sapling yew
to make them bows of the young green wood,
 scorning allegiance due."

The boys were dressed in coarsest cloth,
 bedraggled, weary and cold,
but beneath their hessian stuff there flashed
 a hint of the yellow gold.

They were all besmirched from head to heel
 with mud from the forest floor,
but beneath the grime fair beauty lurked
 and a noble mien they bore.

The barons peered, and they looked again
 and they marvelled at this thing;
then a roar of laughter shook the hall:
 "They are children of the king!"

The ranger looked and he looked again
 and he marvelled at this thing.
"Pardon, sire, I knew not I had bound
 the children of the king."

"Sir Ranger, you have but done your due
 and your fealty I commend,
but the oak and the ash and the sturdy yew
 and the wood from end to end

belong to me and my lusty sons,
 both copse and ride and chase,
and they are the joy of my ageing heart
 and the heirs of all my grace!"

*

O sovereign Lord, to whom all lands,
 all men, all creatures bow,
with our filthy rags and our guilty hands
 and the dirt upon our brow,

we kneel with awe, but we rise with joy
 and with humble thanks we sing;
for we stand complete, we are heirs of grace,
 we are children of the king!

READING JOHN

"It is the custom of the Hebrews to prosecute
more diffusely, afterwards, what they had
touched upon briefly."

                              Calvin, on Genesis 10.10.

Saying the same thing twice
gracefully: that is the art
of Hebrew prose – that is,
Hebrew prose written in Greek.

But in John, not the same
precisely; the same
in a different light
shot with new colours;

the same, as one wave of the sea
is the same as another
but not the same; its thunder
a different note.

Truth, say the waves; truth
drives us; must be obeyed;
the insistent pulse
of the mounting tide

powering each wave further
up the beach, flooding
the mind, driving home
the salt word, further.

ON A DESERT ISLAND

Nearer, my God to thee
might I then feel?

The bleak sand
no stage for vanity;
unkindness having
no victim there;
murder, theft and rape
under that sky
no clay to work on.

Even folly
finding no purpose
would dissolve
in that chaste air.

Surely no warring passions could
destroy that harmony; God
sovereign, nature kind
and, as created
the essential I.

Yet sin, I know
would rage within the heart
harrass the mind
stain the innocent sand
untune the waves
blacken the bright sky.

Part III

WE ARE HIS POEM

Poems of People and Places

FREED

A man leaned out at the world's edge
he stood upon the window ledge.
He smashed the rotting shutters through
he broke the rusted hasp in two.

He flung the creaking window wide
and to the waiting air he cried
"I come, I come, I come to you.
Heaven receive me." And he flew.

He only knew that he was freed
and nothing else. He did not heed
the tiny people crowding round
his broken body on the ground.

ABNORMAL CHILD

He shall be round our necks till the end of time.
We loved him, and desired something splendid,
imagined something great and good. We have hoped
each temper and trial will be ours to harvest;

thought, of each public shame and private rejection,
this is the hardest we shall ever bear;
time will be when the steepest climb is ended;
the last voyage; we shall come at last to harbour.

But perhaps, father, it is time to understand
there will be no answer; be no end of hoping
and the arms that hate you even when they cling
will be round your neck for ever. Time, mother,
to know you are a mother indeed, and had better,
like Mary, find the joy of it here and now.

LITTLE GIDDING

I heard the poem spoken before I read it
(a record). And then I read it later, of course,
and then, as I had to, visited the place.

Voice and verse and place were strangely one.

And now I have read it again. The pigsty, at least,
I understand, and the tomb, and the broken king.
I must soon or never go back to the place again.

KEEP BRITAIN TIDY

"Aren't all human beings natural allies already?"
                        More, *Utopia*, translated by Paul Turner.

Einstein, asked his nationality on entering the USA, said "Human".

"It should be our pride that we are members of the human race rather than of one of its innumerable sub-divisions, but I fear we are not ready for this and doubtless never will be."
                        Peter Ustinov, *Dear Me.*

When *homo* first appeared
the cry went up among the animals
Keep this island natural!

When the Britons came
the cry went up
Iberia for the Iberians!

Hengist and Horsa arrived.
The cry went up
Keep Britain Celtic!

Then the Normans landed.
The cry went up
Keep England Saxon!

The Pakistanis came.
The cry went up
Keep Britain white!

When will the Martians come
and all men cry
Keep Britain human?

JESUS CHRIST, POET

Viola: 'Tis poetical.
Olivia: It is the more like to be feigned.
       Shakespeare, *Twelfth Night.*
Poetry is the parent of superstition.
       Thomas Sprat, founder-member of The Royal Society.
A kind of ingenious nonsense.
       Newton.
         *

There is no greater fiction than that poetry is fiction. Poetry is essentially truthfulness.
       Elizabeth Barrett.

I am sorry for the men of Dryden's age, who thought,
God bless them, poetry was a kind of decoration.
Truth, they believed, was true; science was truth
(Yes, there are many today with the same delusion),
poetry was other. Jesus Christ! Make me patient,
you, the bearer and the being of truth, you
who spoke to women as women, and to children spoke
with eyes and heart, and as man meeting with men,
taught us for all time where poetry is to be found.
Word, living among us today, live among us
and speak to us again, that the name of poet
be no more shamed by syllable-mongers; bare
to the bone our tongue, for poetry, for truth; revive
the go and the gut of real speech, one to one.

FOR BEMERTON

On reading of an appeal for £10,000 to "save George Herbert's Church" in 1977.

Bemerton church is falling down.
    everything cries out, let it fall!
The church has too many mouldy buildings;
    let the weakest go to the wall.
We are busy with radical modernisation,
    synodical government (sure but slow)
and pastoral reorganisation;
    the rural parishes have to go.

And what is the use of those quaint constructions
    Bittersweet, *Giddiness*, *Joseph's Coat* –
crabbed metaphysical speculations?
    we sing today on a different note.
Merely a relic, merely an oddity
    left from an age of mattock and plough –
The Pulley, *The Collar*, *The Quip*, *The Quiddity* –
    nobody reads George Herbert now!

Save the Children, Help the Aged,
    Oxfam, Shelter and Christian Aid
demand their millions; millions give them.
    Love is a debt that is never paid.[1]
But don't let's quibble about ten thousand;
    it's pocket money, it's chicken feed.
Let's see Bemerton church established
    and then to the world with its crying need.

It is one of the small and holy places
    (like Little Gidding) we must not lose,
that speak from the heart to the heart of man
    saying come, be still; and peace; and choose.
Priest, and temple, and *Priest to the Temple*[2]
    the book and the place and the poet forge
a threefold cord that shall not be broken.[3]
    For Bemerton, then, and Holy George.

---

[1] "Love is a personal debt" – George Herbert, *The Church Porch.* Cf. Romans 13.8

[2] Title of Herbert's prose work.

[3] Ecclesiastes 4.12

AT THE FRONTIER

When I stand at Shinjuku[1]
letting five hundred thousand
people walk through my brain
I am at the barrier.

When I step over
the worn threshold
of Ryoanji Temple
I am at the gate.

When I sit cross-legged
on the *tatami* floor
the tea bitter, the talk endless
I am at the door.

When I lie down
unconscious of the speeches
and the heavy flowers
I shall cross the frontier.

---

[1] Tokyo's, perhaps the world's, busiest station

FLOP

In the middle
of my sermon
something like
a ton of putty
fell through
the pulpit floor
smashing the wood
and sinking
out of sight.

I stared.

It was one
of my
platitudes.

A CAROL FOR ST NICHOLAS

"St Nicholas is regarded as the patron saint of sailors…
of children… and also…of Russia… His symbol is
sometimes three bags of gold… Feast day 6 Dec.
Oxford Dictionary of the Christian Church.

As we remember
Nicholas of old,
little though we know,
yet his goodness shines
like beaten gold;

guardian of sailors,
guiding safe to land,
teaching us to feel
through the dark and storm
our Father's hand.

Lover of children,
kind to touch and bless,
gently he restores
the essential grace
of tenderness.

Father of Russia
master of the snow –
through our fellow saints
the eternal God
we love and know.

Shine, saint, and comfort
dark December nights,
pointing to the birth
of the king of kings,
the light of lights.

An original tune is available for this carol.

MORNING AFTER THE ELECTION, 6AM

I'll get up and hear the news.

The sun prepares to keep
his manifesto promise.

The trees have voted
not to renounce their beauty.

The birds seem to think they have won
a substantial majority.

The lawn has not yet lost
its deposit of dew.

Each colour, each party of
creeping things in the grass
has elected to stay.

The results are known,
and the people who starved
yesterday in the Sahel
will starve again tomorrow.

That's settled then.

Now I'll turn on the news.

ABSOLUTELY ALWAYS

"Things absolutely always change for the better"
Peter Preston, editor of *The Guardian*,
in *Third Way*, February 1995.

Things absolutely always
change for the better
said the editor
and he should know;

reporting no doubt
on the Kobe earthquake
football violence
and the growth of AIDS

political corruption
sleaze and rape
live veal exports
and abuse of children.

Someone must have told him
that God is in there somewhere
and things absolutely always
change for the better.

WE WILL REJOICE

"Autou gar esmen poiema – We are his poem"
        Ephesians 2.10
(Written for the silver jubilee of The Fellowship of Christian Writers, 1996)

It is time to rejoice
though the sky seems darker
the road seems rougher
than when we began;
we have made our choice;
let the world shift round us;
we will raise our banner
for God and man.

Twenty-five years
we have kept our faith
we have laughed and prayed;
we were younger then.
We believed in the grace
and the power of God
and through him, the power
and the grace of the pen.

It is time for a modest
celebration
though all we have thought
and seen and heard
is from one source only;
we acknowledge gladly
we are wholly dependent
on the Word.

So let us quietly
give thanks to the maker
for we are his poem;
we have made our choice.
We will – though humbly
though well aware
of the darkness – we will,
we will rejoice.

DOME'S DAY

I will praise the dome,
since all men laugh at it.

When I walk the City I marvel,
banks, theatres, churches, crowned
with magnificent domes;
a solar system of hemispheres
centred on Paul's,
an orrery of bright invention.

As a boy I loved
the Dome of Discovery.

In the fields I find mushrooms;
I see many clouds, trees,
some hills, some barrows,
flowers everywhere
domed with beauty.

The brain I need
to write with ticks snugly
in its dome-shaped house of bone,
made in the living image
of its creator.

The creator
starting from scratch
prized apart matter and matter,
making a floor of walkable earth
roofed with a visible dome[1]
which declares his glory.[2]

Let us have our hemisphere
though the globe demands us.

We will pour out our love
till the end of our days
on the crying of the world
till jubilee come;
but let us have our dome
for the measuring of time.

Though all men laugh at it
I will praise the dome.

---

[1] Genesis 1.6
[2] Psalm 19.1

SHELTERED ACCOMMODATION

I suppose the story begins
when desire grows warm, and the exact
virility slides home, perfectly
sheltered, perfectly accommodated
in the one-flesh fulfilment
of the master plan.

Follows the safe home
of the new soul, cushioned
like a conker in pulpy protection,
nine months tenancy providing
sheltered accommodation
for the little treasure.

Follows the rough
century of experience;
little shelter there
until the planed oak
neatly fits the case,
the lining soft and snug
as the undertaker can make it.

But finally
the last and forever lasting
sheltered accommodation
wraps the soul with singing.
The light perfectly meets
the body and its demands.
Man goes to his long home,
entrance is free, and the resident
warden never fails.

SIXTEEN

Tracey, sixteen
on the table, sweats
crucified by pain.
Push now, they say.
Bastards. I can't.
Where's Steve?
Life has never been like this.
Deep breaths.
I can't. Get Steve!
Push now.
I can't.
Now.

Steve, sixteen, unaware
balancing his beer
on the edge of the table
seriously considers
coming off the cushion
behind the yellow
to find the middle pocket.

Or should he go for safety?

The decision
is agonising.
He chalks his cue, breathing;
becomes a father by default.

JOSHUA CHAPTER 3

Bridge and *ferry* are words
not found in holy writ.

No such worldly things
intrude in Israel's story.

Civil engineering would be
such a denial of faith!

The great mathematician
is the great engineer.

Let him divide the waters;
really so much simpler.

THREE CHILDREN OF THE KING

Three boys, serving beauty, began
their quest. And the true lovers,
the secret servants of the king, found joy
in the venture these three embarked upon,
seeking the kingdom: Jack and Charles and John.

Following their lord, they found grace;
serving truth, built landscapes of the heart,
colours of the mind, ink on the page, giving joy
to millions; sought the far kingdom and brought back
treasures for us all – Charles, and John, and Jack.

They illumined the animal world; restored wonder,
Resolved the semantics of romance. Moreover
Kept the way of the king who called for children
To make up his cause, taking his young blood, led
By his spirit; like Arthur, somewhat childgered.

They defied academia, sat loose to power; Jack, now,
in Narnia, shared the gift; Charles, under the mercy,
place of the lion, drew his last breath in surrender
to the beauty that had possessed him. John gave birth
to a world of amazement in and over Middle Earth.

Lights of the last century, stay with us,
Charles and Jack and John. We need you.
Our childhood in danger, like a cup of water carried
over broken ground, cries out for your comforting.
Restore innocence. Lead us to the king.

This poem celebrates the works of romance and fantasy in the Christian tradition by three 20th century writers, Charles Williams (1886-1945), JRR (John) Tolkien (1892-1973) and CS (Jack) Lewis (1898-1963).

Line 12 CS Lewis analyses seven meanings of the word *romance* in the Preface to *The Pilgrim's Regress* (1933).

Line 15 *childgered*, a Middle English word applied to the young King Arthur in the 14th century *Sir Gawayn and the Grene Knycht*, means boyish, restless, hot-blooded – a quality that would perhaps have appealed to all three of our authors.

Line 17 *Under the mercy* is carved on Charles Williams' gravestone in the churchyard of St Cross, Holywell, Oxford.

Lines 18-19 An echo of a sentence in Williams' *The Place of the Lion*: "...as twilight began to fall, her father drew his last breath in final surrender to the beauty that had possessed him."

Line 20 *Middle Earth* was the name Tolkien gave to his imaginary world.

TRUTH AND BEAUTY

"Beauty is truth, truth beauty – that is all
ye know on earth, and all ye need to know."

Well, Johnny Keats – agreed. Your bluff I call.
Jesus is truth and beauty. It is so.

Part IV

COMING HOME

Poems of time and eternity

APOCALYPSE

All winter white
all summer green
we suffer birth
we kindly die

guiding our flight
midway between
the trusty earth
and the fickle sky.

Come, trumpet blast
come darkness; send
the driving gales
the flying rains.

We stand aghast
at the year's end.
the earth fails
and the sky remains.

HUMPH

> ... poets
> ... the tongues of Pentecost
> Their privilege...
>
> Victoria Sackville-West, *The Land*

Don't be afraid. For the way
is common, the gate easy.
In greeth we are going, and together
we jorn, we will freely open
barls, corbins and all, for the double
trode of beeling, transfetted
grale peewins. Lost! We are knee-dock
in swithun wellons awash
lithe farling gopher and zoogreet
for all we can clumbridge darly.
Min swiggle to every rathbinch
swavely, swavely torbroke
wen deening bradsin vone-ark
glow priscable sharn from blors.
Lee doffgose, gratulous swinchap
insarbling the crost calpindus
filijote, adda lowgrid menswing
we dorjin yarely, yarely.
otis in axlip, lordlife
sween graze-art fractible, poonish
fraise dilwich, and wexith milgrom
we darvilly brinvoe dench.
For this wint sordil enorpid
I vaise and dwensuch spander
we give what walfash leers
doriman, each stoven in bailest
hellstar. For glowdark and infill
and self, this pretect fission
we lornwill maiding praise.

ONE WAY

My years are passing now, and I walk the road
of no return.
> Job 16.22 (Good News Bible)

We drive a one-way system.
Thank goodness.

On the motorway
there are no u-turns.
Just as well.

At the tube station
those flapping doors
fly open at a touch
and close again.

The escalator
carries me to the gate;
no turning back.

In the supermarket
the turnstile allows
no second thoughts.
So be it.

We have such lessons then.
My years are passing
now, and I walk
the road of no return.

CROWN HIM LORD OF ALL

"In him are hidden all the treasures of wisdom and knowledge."
   Colossians 2.3

I meditate on Jesus
transcendentally.

Astrology leads me to the birth
of Jesus the morning star.

Islam is submission to Jesus.

Nirvana is the kingdom of Jesus.

Animism bows to Jesus as lord.

Theosophy is Jesus,
the power and wisdom of God.

Judaism is Jesus full stop.

Zen asks. Jesus answers.

Yoga sits. Jesus rules.

Communism is the dialectic of Jesus.

Jesus is the friend of the earth.

Jesus brings in the new age.

HERE HE COMES

Pipe him aboard
salute
dip colours
present arms.
Arches
banners
tickertape
balloons.
Parade
procession
march-past
walkabout.
Red carpet
a banquet
a bouquet
a fanfare.
Beacons
bonfires
cannons
fireworks.
Shouts
and smiles
and flags
and things.
Welcome
Jesus
king
of kings.

SUPERFICIAL

I am a superficial person.
Thank God.

Being superficial
is super.

I skate
on the surface
like nononecta glauca.

I don't pretend
to be God.

One day
I will be drowned
and sink into life
totally immersed,
celebrating
the solid quiet
all around.

But let's keep that
for eternity.

I'll get death over first.

TIME

Time flies.
Nothing wonderful there.
So do swifts, beetles and dragonflies.

We haven't got time.
Time has got us, the great bully,
when the clocks chime.

Time is the great healer
so they say; also the great sharper,
shuffler and dealer.

Time is running out
and round and round in circles
and in again no doubt.

Time marches on,
oh yes, and off, and on,
and off, and on.

Only time will tell
but rumour, gossip and slander
do the job as well.

Time and time again
time, the poor sod, tries to answer
the question when.

What do you make the time?
I make the time do what I want it to;
serve this rhyme.

Time gentlemen please.
They all say that. So much
for the law and its decrees.

Just in time, if we must;
sometimes, and sometimes not;
and sometimes unjust.

For the time being, tit for tat,
we will go on living,
if you can call it that.

Once upon a time
the story is terrific,
the ending sublime.

Time's up
like the knife in the wound,
the last arrow, the bitter cup.

It's time to go
out into the windy dark
and the driving snow.

I was killing time yesterday
and I killed him. So there.
Everybody shout hurray.

COMMONLY CALLED LIFE

Perhaps between
arrival and dispatch,
between delivery and committal,
this giddy ride
is all we can expect;

a brief and breathless
interlude, laced
with danger, an episode
freighted with fear;

a diversion from steadiness,
a secular escape;

until the coasting wheels
rest, the ride is over,
and life resumes
its proper course.

THE STREAM OF TIME

As glides the stream
in summer, where the willow falls
in a half dream
by shady flower-cascading walls,

and gentle boats
slip sweetly down the laughing river;
the lily floats,
the water flows in peace for ever,

and distant bells
across the pasture call and chime
through leafy dells -
so glides the flowing stream of time

bearing us on
through fitful showers and dappled shadow
and sudden sun
past reeds and grasses, field and meadow,

till the great leap
of plunging waters widen free
into the deep,
their home at last. The sea! The sea!